Reflections Of Life

A collection of poetry and verse inspired by nature,

life, love and loss.

Trish Abbott

Credits

All Pictures © Trish Abbott, 2020 with the exception of:

Early Morning Hare	© Harry Read
Magical Woodland Glade	© Kate Moore
Life's Pathway	© Alan Simpson
Sunset In Motion	© Polly Thorpe
Morning Mist	© Robert Newton
Mystical Gateway	© Lynda Simpson
Across The Sea	© Ben Tizard
After The Storm	© Ray McBride
Twilight Scene	© Malcolm Matheson
A New Dawn Beginning	© Beccy Dewing
Fading Sunset	© Chris Dewing
Summer Mist	© Miranda Avery
Lost In Solitude	© Peter Heal
Beauty Of Summer	© Alan Simpson
Mother Nature's Portrait	© Granville Girdlestone
Sharing Special Moments	© Emma Gampell
Sunset Reflections	© Alan Simpson
Pathway To The Beach	© Gary Pearson
A Golden Sunrise	© Les Jarrald
Moments In Time	© Granville Girdlestone
Evening Across The Fens	© Ian Robinson
My Special Secret Place	© Jackie Suttling
After Dusk	© Barry Rasberry
Last Light	© Mandy Hudson
Autumn Reflections	© Julie Marshall
The Cromer Crab Man	© Brad Damms
Morning Flight	© Brad Damms
The Force Of Nature	© Ray McBride
Reflections Of The Sea	© Paul Carter
Just A Perfect Day	© Lors Birnie
Fire And Ice	© Simon Gray
Nature's Keyhole	© Lynz Vincent
Echoes On The Beach	© Katie Morgan
Standing Alone	© Stuart Hill

Dedication

This collection of poetry and verse is lovingly dedicated to my brave husband and soulmate Phil Abbott, who lost his fight to Prostate Cancer on his 67th birthday, 4 June 2018. It was too short a time between his diagnosis and his passing, but the amazing way he coped with it (and me) with humour and dignity, is something that I will always be in awe of, and he will always be my hero.

For the last 4 years Phil had been encouraging me to publish my work, and although the idea was there, I never really found the time to get the ball rolling.

Now sadly I seem to have a lot of spare time, so, my darling, the love of my life, I am creating this for you.

The profits from the sales of this book will be donated to Prostate Cancer UK in the hope that they will find new ways to diagnose, and successfully treat those who are still here to reap the benefits.

Table of Contents

Foreword by Tony Collier

Foreword

By Tony Collier

Since Trish lost her Husband to the awful illness that is prostate cancer she has been totally dedicated, not just to Phil's memory but to supporting other men and their families who are living with prostate cancer whilst trying to save men's lives by spreading awareness and raising funds for Prostate Cancer UK.

As a man living with stage 4, terminal, prostate cancer I really appreciate everything that Trish does to support men like me and help prolong our lives.

Her poetry is stunning, poignant, happy and sometimes sad but always uplifting and glorious. I'm sure her book will be a resounding success and I'm absolutely honoured to be asked to write this foreword.

Raising awareness is so vital for a disease that isn't screened for especially when most men diagnosed have no symptoms at all. Trish's work will help to save men not having to go through what her and her family have been through and I wish her huge success.

#men, we are with you.

Tony Collier BEM

Trish Abbott

Early Morning Hare

As morning breaks and brings the light, another new day dawns
On frozen earth so hard and cold she rests upon the lawn

The sunlight penetrates her skin and soaks away the chill
So reluctant to be on the move she sits alone and still

She doesn't see us watching as she waits for time to pass
While diamonds sparkle in the sun on frosty blades of grass

Across her path the spiders spin their webs of golden thread
They shimmer in the morning sun above her bended head

We wonder just how long she'll stay before she turns to run
And lope across the fields of white beneath the warming sun

Trish Abbott

Magical Woodland Glade

Sunlight brings a warming glow amidst the woodland glade
A place that's full of mystery where fairy tales are made

Imagine those who make their home in tangled roots of trees
Collecting leaves and sturdy twigs to hold up tiny eaves

The soft green moss they gather up to make a comfy bed
And sip their tea from acorn cups, made out of berries red

If you sit down and do not move you may just get a peek
Of tiny folk and other little creatures that you seek

Please do not cough or make a noise to frighten them away
Remain quite still and watch with joy as out they come to play

They spread their gossamer rainbow wings to warm in golden rays
Whilst singing secret magical songs that tell of olden days

And just as quickly as they come, they disappear once more
Beneath the shade of grassy stems that grow on woodland floor

Trish Abbott

Life's Pathway

We walk along life's earthly path not knowing where it leads

While parts of it are smooth and flat, there's bumpy bits indeed

Some obstacles seem hard to move and stop us in our tracks

But when we find solutions they reveal their hidden cracks

Reflections of the bright blue sky that dazzle with its view

Are blurred as ripples in the pools disturb the picture's hue

Instead of uphill struggles why not take each step with smiles

We start to find an easy route with every passing mile

This open road will teach us ways to make our time fulfilling

And show us many other paths to take, If we are willing

And although the walk brings challenges with every slippery slope

Let's follow it regardless with determined joy and hope

Trish Abbott

Sunset In Motion

The silky golden haze that shines a pathway to the shore

Where pebbles sit like burnished coins upon a sandy floor

As sea birds fly together in the hope to catch some fry

That dart beneath the foamy waves below the dusky sky

Their silhouette-like shadows bold and stark above the land

While bubbling surf below them washes through the grains of sand

Deep royal blue and purple floats above the sparkling bay

Like a gentle cloak descending as we bid farewell to day

And pretty soon the sun will sink to welcome back the night

These birds will settle down and wait for early morning light

A darkened veil will sweep across while colours fade to black

Revealing silver moon and stars to light our homeward track

Trish Abbott

Morning Mist

A golden globe hangs in the sky amongst the eerie mist
It's risen to embrace us with its early morning kiss

Reflecting in the ripples as they spread across the lake
Arousing all within its warming touch, and gentle wake

Shadows of the landscape show themselves beneath the cloud
The soft and muted background peering through its misty shroud

The sound of daytime greetings from the wildlife all around
Breathes life into the stillness of the water and the ground

Then slowly while we watch in awe, the vision changes view
As diamonds start to sparkle on the sunlit drops of dew

And misty wisps will slowly swirl then gently fade way
Leaving images of magic on this new unfolding day

Trish Abbott

Mystical Gateway

What lies beyond this wooden gate's a mystery to us all

All overgrown with fauna, camouflaged and standing tall

And yet it seems inviting me to lift its rusty latch

Whilst pushing up against the boards to see if they will catch

There may be hidden treasure troves beyond these walls of brick

Or a magic secret garden with its lawn so lush and thick

A place where sparkling fountains fall into a misty pool

Where water flows between the rocks to caverns dark and cool

I think I hear some birdsong, so maybe there are trees?

An orchard full of blossoms pink that float upon the breeze

Who knows what wonders could be seen if I just peep inside

But should I enter through the gate?, I really can't decide

Trish Abbott

Across The Sea

Who stops to sit upon this bench that overlooks the sea?

Maybe a weary walker rests to rub a tired knee

Or could it be a favourite place to pause and see the views?

A special seat at evening time to banish daytime blues

Perhaps an invitation to reflect your thoughts that day

While getting lost in memories, the time just slips away

Two lovers linger hand in hand entwined within the glow.

The two are one, no need for words they let their feelings show

A peaceful place to read a book while listening to the shore

The waves a gentle whispering are calling "come, explore"

And whatever reason calls upon the need to stop and stare

Be sure to stay a little while enjoying all that's there

Trish Abbott

After The Storm

An afternoon of storms and rain leaves stunning evening views
Of apricots and dusky mauves, with pretty shades of blues
The wispy clouds of smoky grey that spread across the sky
Are reflected in the water like a mirror, where they lie

An eerie light falls on the scene as storm clouds move away
A breeze sweeps through the rigging causing boats to gently sway
It whispers through the mooring ropes that hold the vessels fast
Creating sounds of chinking as it stirs in sail and mast

Then colours dull and fade away as daytime turns to night
The ever changing landscape fills our senses with delight
But distant rolling thunder warns the storm is still around
And rain will softly fall once more upon the misty ground

Twilight Scene

Velvet skies emerge as the day begins to close

Muted purples mix with the pink of a rose

Quiet water shimmering so still and very deep

Softly as a whisper while we gently fall asleep

Night time slowly creeping is just a breath away

Dulling all the colours and the pale fading rays

Shadows are appearing like a cool dark veil

Flowing gently round us with their misty trail

Then tiny stars come out to play and twinkle in the sky

The night time takes us over as we bid the day goodbye

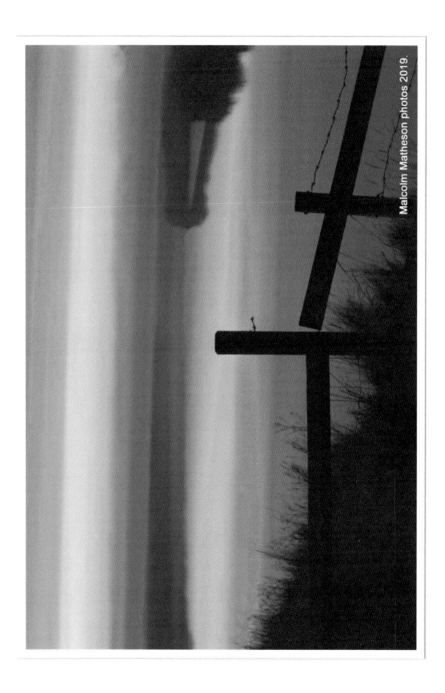

Malcolm Matheson photos 2019.

Trish Abbott

Emerging Into Spring

It starts out kind of slowly when spring begins to show

The snowdrops raise their tiny heads above the melting snow

Then yellow flowering aconite and crocus, mauve and blue

A picture perfect carpet in the sparkling morning dew

The mad March hares are bounding out across the fields of green

Whilst rabbits chase each other round the hedgerows in between

And in the woods a sea of bluebells fill the ground with ease

Their nodding bells waft perfume in the warm and gentle breeze

Below them purple violets splashing colour as they grow

Picked out in dappled sunlight, they create a stunning show

The sound of birdsong fills the air in treetops high above

Telling everyone around them that their hearts are filled with love

Then as you take a fragranced breath and feel the warming sun

The memory of the winter fades while new life has begun

So pause here for a moment, let the warmth caress your face

When its springtime in the countryside, there is no better place

Trish Abbott

A New Dawn Beginning

As the bells ring out the old year, they're bringing in the new

A shifting of vibrations meaning change for me and you

Time to start afresh again, to leave the "old" behind

Thoughts of new exciting plans, and lessons for mankind

Less focus on material things allows our minds to grow

Please worry not what people say, we'll reap what we will sow

A welcome journey to embrace, new pathways etched in earth

With friendships formed and lessons learned, it's almost like re-birth

We shine a beam of guiding light so others find their way

While Some can heal, and others teach, assisting every day

Our nurtured souls respond with joy, and shoulders shed their load

As we take the first of many steps along life's unmade road

Together we can build new lives, bring hope to where we go

Where all of us can merge to share this healing energy flow

So ring out the old and bring in the new, march on without a fear

Towards a new and brighter life, to welcome our new year

Trish Abbott

My Fairies

What was that? a sparkle in the sky
Or was it a fairy that was just passing by?
I'm sure I really saw her, it wasn't in a dream,
In the blink of an eyelid she was almost nearly seen

At the bottom of my garden in a small wooded glade
The fairies are all living in the homes that they've made
In tiny little houses whittled out of woodland trees,
Or in pretty toadstool dwellings that have tiny little eaves

They shelter from the rain, or so I am told,
Under leaves and ferns or blades of grass, to keep from getting cold
But when the sun comes out again they dart amongst the flowers,
Sipping nectar from the tiny bells filled up from April showers

At night they are so busy as we dream the darkness through
Sprinkling fairy dust upon us so our wishes will come true
And in the light as dawn appears back to the glade they fly,
To sleep, or dance, or sing their songs, and eat some acorn pie

Trish Abbott

Angel In The Sky

Floating in the clear blue sky I gaze upon an angel's wing
To most it's just a passing cloud; a shape, and not a special thing

To me the pictures framed by blue, are signs from angels up above
Their lovely shapes bring hope and joy, sent down to us with warmth and love

And sometimes I see feathery shapes, they float in view for all to see
A message from someone so dear? A sign to say "Its' really me"

I know they watch to keep us safe, and guide us as we find our way
A picture sign to show they care, a loving hug just makes our day

And all too soon they fade, or change to other shapes that paint the sky
But keep on looking, they are there! Your angel friends that float close by

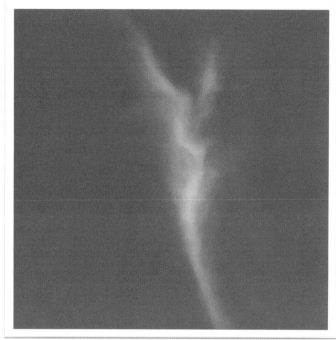

Fading Sunset

The sun that sets and fades away
brings closure to a summer's day
Pink and turquoise gold and red,
a stunning scene for the night ahead

The mist is falling all around
and dampening down the cooling ground
As the night time bats will stir and fly
leaving silhouettes in the evening sky

While creatures rest at the end of the day
in a comfy place all amongst the hay
This picture changes all too soon
as the velvety cloak reveals the moon

And tiny stars that sparkle bright
show a different scene in the indigo night
The foreground fades and the shadows spread,
it's time for home and a comfy bed

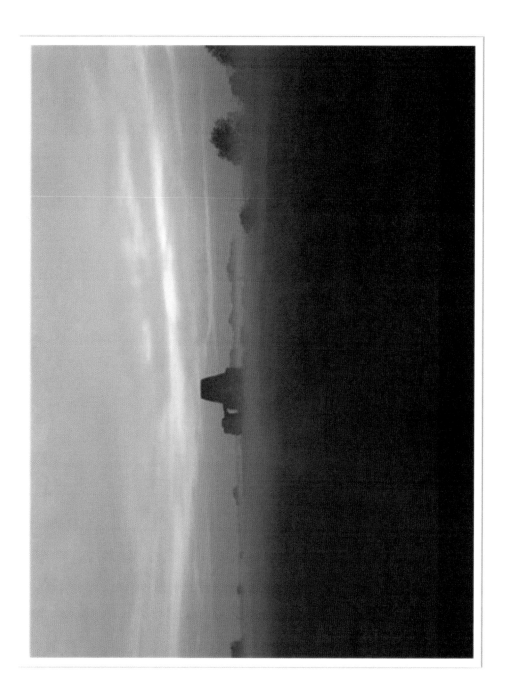

Trish Abbott

Harvest Time

Harvest time is busy as we gather up the grain

Making sure it's safely dry from sudden bursts of rain

Golden rolls of barley straw will soon be stacked up high

A bountiful good harvest underneath the summer sky

We thank you dearest Mother Earth for nurturing our land

And celebrate this fruitful time together hand in hand.

Trish Abbott

Summer Mist

The mist across the meadow brings a closure to my day

While the shadows on the trees grow dark as daytime slips away

Pretty pinks and muted blues reflect the setting sun

And I feel a coolness in the air as night time has begun

Birds will flock to find their roosts and settle for the night

As the velvet cloak of darkness slowly dims and fades the light

But for now I sit in silence while I gaze upon this land,

Watching nature paint her picture with such beauty in her hands

Trish Abbott

Lost In Solitude

Waves crashing down on the sand and stone,

I listen to the roar as I sit here alone

Echoes in the shells as the sea draws back

Whispering "come follow" in their foamy track

Warming sun caresses from the deep blue sky

As soft breezes dry away the tears from my eyes

Breathing in the salty air and cool sea spray

Reflecting on the thoughts that embrace me today

Reluctant to leave as the clouds gather round,

Thunder in the distance is a threatening sound

I will return tomorrow just to sit here once more

Getting lost in solitude upon this golden sandy shore

Trish Abbott

Beauty Of Summer

Looking far across the meadow out towards the trees and sky
Shadows grey above the flowers from the clouds that float on by
Patches form of blood red poppies mingled with the blooms of gold
Summer greens of bush and hedgerow helps this picture to unfold

Shapes appear within the clouds that glide across the skies of blue
Changing form they shift their patterns altering the picture's view
Grasses bending in the breeze with gentle warmth from summer sun
Spreading out to far horizon where the land and sky are one

Trees that stand along the edges give some shade to all below
Leafy boughs that rustle softly, spread their branches as they grow
Nature has revealed her beauty in its glory, wild and free
Captured here and shared together bringing joy for all to see

Trish Abbott

Peaceful Water's Edge

Sitting in the summer sun I feel the warming rays soak in
With just a gentle calming breeze that whispers cool upon my skin
Gazing out across the water, sparkling ripples catch my eye.
Reflections in the rocky pools that mirror back the deep blue sky

Iris blooms of gold and blue grow tall along the shallow edge
Where water mint and clover pink fill spaces on the rocky ledge
Swallows dive to sip the water as I sit beneath the trees
Dappled sunlight gold and silver dance between their soft green leaves

I close my eyes and tilt my face to greet the warming sunlight glow
And breathe in perfume from the flowers, given freely as they grow
It feels so good to sit in silence, not a word needs to be said
Nature's beauty all around me. Thoughts of summer fill my head

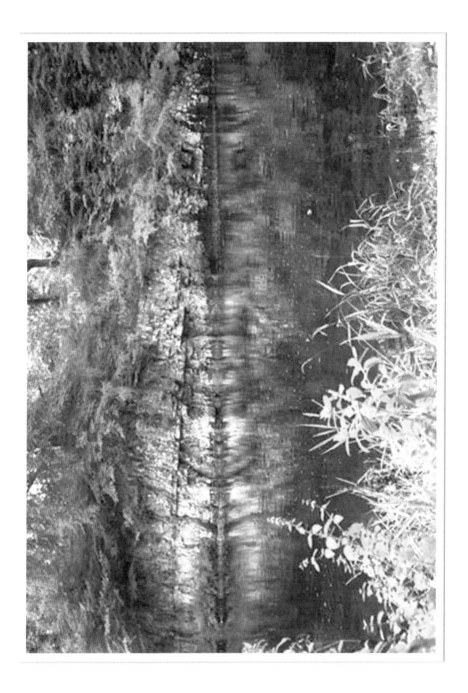

Mother Nature's Portrait

Shadows deepen in the mist as all to soon the daytime ends

The Solitary hoot of a lonely bird calling out to finds its friends

A Tangerine globe descending down behind the dark and cloudy sky

Leaves remnants of a sunny day, that sadly now has passed on by

The blue mist hangs so cool and damp its moist breath stirs the evening air

As night time covers trees and fields to gently darken everywhere

Such beauty can be captured in the blinking of a human eye

While watching Mother Nature paint her perfect portrait in the sky

Trish Abbott

Sharing Special Moments

Stay a while and let us ponder by the water's whispering reeds
As this day prepares to slumber, warm and peaceful it recedes

Gentle breezes reaching out to bathe our skin with sweet caress
Dappled sunlight in the grasses, sparkling through its tangled mess

Burnished gold reflecting water, ripples spread to reach the edge
Sounds of creatures softly calling, birds return to tree and hedge

Very soon the setting sun will change the view that we now see
Ruby reds replace the yellows, deep rich purples flowing free

As our thoughts begin to wander, we prepare to make our way
Footsteps tread familiar pathways, sharing memories of the day

Trish Abbott

Sunset Reflections

This golden clear horizon brings a closing to the day

It shines across the tranquil sea to where the pebbles lay

Like tiny scattered jewels they all sparkle in the sand

Dropped along the shoreline out of Mother Nature's hand

While cobalt blue and turquoise paint a portrait way up high

A background to dramatic clouds that sweep across the sky

And gentle shadows on the rocks that nestle down below

Will wash across the surface like a muted silver throw

Our view will soon become obscured as dusk and dark appears

An ever changing picture as the evening time draws near

When chilly air blows in our face we will prepare to roam

To seek the warmth and comfort from our very welcomed home

Trish Abbott

Pathway To The Beach

A long and narrow pathway that runs beside the shore

Is trodden down by footsteps of those who walked before

An endless sky of vivid blue as far as eyes can see

With fluffy clouds like cotton wool that float ahead of me

And grassy dunes that line the path wave gently in the breeze

They whisper softly, "stop a while to gaze across the sea"

I feast my eyes upon the scene, a panoramic view

Out to the far horizon steeped in shades of green and blue

The sea of sparkling sapphires sending ripples to the land

As gentle waves caress the beach of soft and golden sand

While sun shines warm upon my face and fills me with delight

For time has stopped as I enjoy the beauty of this sight

Trish Abbott

A Golden Sunrise

Willows weep at start of daybreak, dewy tears fall in the pool
Gold reflecting in the sunrise, all around us feeling cool
Mist is rising from the grasses, promise of a warm new day
Ripples spread across the water, fish swim up to feed and play

Breezes whisper in the branches, moving through the leaves of green
Gently swaying back and forwards, leaving shadows where they've been
Cattle lowing in the distance, sounding lost and quite forlorn
Birdsong fills the air with music, drifting through the misty dawn

Hazy sunlight soft like butter, spreads across the summer sky
Wispy clouds on far horizon, making shapes as they drift by
Each new day as light emerges, brings us all a special treat
Every scene is always different, nature's palette is complete

Moments In Time

Golden shafts of sunlight flow through holes in silver cloud

Just beneath the velvet cloak of evening's darkening shroud

The molten bronze reflections shimmer right across the bay

Whilst bobbing craft like silhouettes just gently rock and sway

Behind the fiery water are the hills that rise up high

A dark and rolling backdrop reaching up towards the sky

They cast out eerie shadows as the eventide draws near

That creep towards the golden shore to join the water clear

And so taken by the beauty of the colour's softened hues

We gaze in breathless wonder at the ever changing views

We capture one last picture showing nature's perfect light

Before it fades completely as the daytime turns to night

Trish Abbott

Evening Across The Fens

The golden sun is setting at the ending of the day
Whispering across the fen, the breezes seem to say
"Turn sails turn" they softly call, but sadly no reply
They stand as still as statues in the evening cloud lit sky

Then orange sunrays disappear, the colour palette changes
With purple streaks and indigos as nature re-arranges
While night time creatures venture out to wander far and near
An owl will hoot and fox will bark to warn that they are here

Soon the velvet darkness of the night encloses round
Mists will fall like curtains on the cool and dampened ground
And welcomed fires will be lit to warm the autumn night
As smoky swirling silhouettes stand out in fading light

Trish Abbott

My Special Secret Place

I found this scene the other day whilst walking in the wood

It sort of took my breath away; was rooted where I stood

The gold and ambers of the leaves all scattered on the ground

Reflected on the surface of the water all around

And once my feet were mine again I walked the leafy track

To find a place to sit awhile before I ventured back

The stillness of the air around, I breathed in long and deep

It was so peaceful sitting there, a memory made to keep

To merge with Mother Nature I removed my socks and shoes

Encompassed by the colours, I absorbed their shades and hues

The feeling of the crispy leaves felt good beneath my feet

Whilst sunshine warmth was on my face, I felt its gentle heat

Amazing birdsong filled the air from treetops high above

Their calling song so beautiful it filled my heart with love

How wonderful it was to spend an afternoon of pleasure

By chance to find this secret place is something I will treasure

Trish Abbott

After Dusk

The eerie mist is rising as it spreads across the ground

Like pastel coloured candy floss that doesn't make a sound

Reflections from the setting sun reveals an amber glow

A backdrop to the shadow of the trees that stand below

Cobwebs hang from wiry posts like lacy jewelled beads

That reach across to decorate the grass and nearby reeds

But soon the stillness of the night will change this picture's view

When shrouds of darkness envelope the skies of gold and blue

Then Autumn chills descend upon the damp and moistened land

And crackling fires call us from the place where now we stand

We wrap our coats around us and decide to make our way

With memories of the special place we shared with you today

Trish Abbott

Last Light

Peeking through the grasses tall, I focus on the view
Stormy shadows in the sky reflect the golden hue

Violet clouds are gathering above the sun so low
Mirrored from a palette in the water down below

The warmth that did caress my skin, I feel it cooling fast
As darkness soon will dim the scene that evening shadows cast

If time stood still for just a while, I could enjoy some more
And bathe in colours rich and bold, a pleasure I adore

So I try to capture everything and place it in my mind
Before I turn to journey home and leave the day behind

Trish Abbott

Autumn Reflections

Pausing for a morning break along the lakeside shore
Treading leaves already fallen crisp on woodland floor

Hazy sunshine filters through and highlights all around
Muted shadows in the trees stretch out across the ground

As tangled branches stooping over, lean to water's edge
Reflecting softly like a mirror etched on glassy ledge

The canopy of living green will turn to shades of gold
And slowly drift on Autumn breeze to rest as leafy mould

A sanctuary of calm and peace that soaks in through the skin
Imprinting thoughts and happy memories captured deep within

Trish Abbott

The Cromer Crab Man

Evening calls the lonesome boatman

Fishing day is almost done

Drop the final baskets over

Sail to shore through golden sun

Feeling warmth across his shoulders

Gentle breeze caress his face

Bobbing softly in the water

Cherished moments of this place

Bringing home the daily bounty

Fresh delicious Cromer crabs,

Langoustines and feisty lobsters

Flounders, plaice and silver dabs

Molten waves that glow and shimmer

Like a path of silken thread

Leading back to welcomed harbour

Thoughts of food and comfy bed

Trish Abbott

Morning Flight

The geese are flying over at the breaking of the dawn

Reflecting in the water as another day is born

While silken gold that brightens up the early morning sky

Creates a warming outline to the clouds that float on by

Shades of mauve and lavender blend in with turquoise blue

Evoking special feelings of our early morning view

The grasses gently waving as they're touched by cooling breeze

They bend and sway like dancers moving slowly and with ease

Each day begins uniquely, it's so different every time

As Mother Nature offers us a gift that's so sublime

And feeling very humble as we feast upon this scene

Agreeing that today is quite the best it's ever been

Trish Abbott

The Force Of Nature

When rainfall flows into the lake it soon becomes a flood

As country roads are all awash with rivulets of mud

But after there's a calmness as the beauty is revealed

And so quiet is the water as it slowly claims the fields

The silver ripples spread towards a new created shore

Where once there was a footpath, sadly "out of use" once more

And mountains form a backdrop to this peaceful northern lake

With snowy peaks that sparkle like the frosting on a cake

A gate and fence the only clue that land was ever there

Whilst a mirror-like reflection seems to make us want to stare

And the muted pinks and lilacs let us know the day is done

Leaving memories of the magic with the setting of the sun

Trish Abbott

Reflections Of The Sea

I sit in awe and wonder as I gaze across the sea
The waves are crashing round the rocks; I feel the spray on me
A molten globe of golden sun descends to watery grave
That leaves a glowing shoreline as it's lost beneath the waves

Reflections in the shallow pools of coppery orange fire
Feels gently warm upon my face which lift my spirits higher
So I close my eyes and listen to the surf upon the sand
It rushes through the pebbles, singing tunes of sea and land

And becoming so absorbed within, there is no time or space
At one with my surroundings and the beauty of this place
I capture every moment as the day begins to fade
Creating special memories that the afternoon has made

Trish Abbott

Nature's Showers

We have enjoyed the sunshine, the sunny skies of blue

But looking at the dusty ground some rain is overdue

As darkness creeps across the day and rain begins to fall

It drops towards the needy earth and soaks the trees so tall

And birds will bathe in puddles, fluffing feathers as they clean

Then find themselves a covered branch where they can safely preen

While the tiny insects shelter from the heavy drops of rain

They hope it won't be long before the sun comes out again

As children pull their wellies on and make a hurried dash

They squeal with joy whilst jumping in the puddles with a splash!

And dogs find muddy ditches, to wallow, roll and play

Then leave the smelly water on our carpets where they lay

The earth will still keep turning and the sun will rise and set

And clouds will drift across the sky above the land now wet

Remember too the sun will shine once more to warm our skin

As nature's show continues to bring beauty from within

Trish Abbott

Just A Perfect Day

The sun is disappearing down below the Scottish land

A tree stands in the foreground like a fragile waving hand

We watch the clouds change colour as they catch the evening glow

Reflecting on the water like a mirror down below

Orange, pink and turquoise spread across the sky so bright

While the mountains in the distance bid the setting sun goodnight

Rising high above the water with their snowy laden caps

And the clouds drift slowly over as their shadows fill the gaps

Then molten silky ripples wash the pebbles on the shore

They shine like golden treasure that's been scattered on the floor

A cooling evening mist will soon be dampening our clothes

And crackling fires call us home to warm our chilly toes

Trish Abbott

Fire And Ice

Crashing waves against the rocks that never seem to tire

While on the clear horizon glows a golden line of fire

Reflecting orange rays to show the ending of the day

Captured in the splashes of the salty ice cold spray

And clouds that gather silently across the evening sky

Bring a warning of refreshing rain before the night goes by

But just for now let us enjoy what nature has to show

Foamy pools that flow round rock and soak the sand below

We listen to the roaring sea which sounds like paradise

As the setting sun across wet stone resembles fire and ice

Trish Abbott

Nature's Keyhole

Take a peek through nature's keyhole and reveal what is to see

As we stumble on a secret through the clumps of sturdy trees

Crispy ferns snap underneath us, crackling as we gently tread

While this glade of glowing colour filters through the gap ahead

Burnished gold and deepest orange brightly flowing into view

Shooting fiery little pathways bold amongst the misty dew

All around feels still and silent up above the golden light

Shadows filled with eerie darkness pushing daylight into night

So we move a little closer just to feel its warming glow

Bathing in the liquid amber as we step towards its flow

While we capture all the magic that we may not see again

As in time it fades to darkness, only memories will remain

Trish Abbott

Echoes On The Beach

We will remember them 1914 - 2014

Across the dunes of whispering winds, a hundred years have passed

Since our good lads were marched away, the battle raging fast

They looked so brave but underneath their fear was locked inside

The echoes of their hobnail boots together stride for stride

For some their boots would not be treading back on homeland soil

The rolling tide would wash away the endless blood and toil

These poppies are a bold red sign reflecting all around

A patch of colour standing out upon the trodden ground

Upon this night we will be still and light a candle flame

Remembering the fate of those whose imprint still remain

And in our thoughts with heartfelt pride for those who are no more

We hope their fight for peace and love, be welcome on this shore

Trish Abbott

Standing Alone

We will remember them

He stood out tall and on his own when all around was grey
Unsure of what would happen as he slowly marched away

And left behind the barley fields of his beloved land
While others followed in his steps to swell the loyal band

They left their homes and families so proud and oh so brave
Believing in their heart of hearts their country they could save

But bloody battles took their toll and some of them were lost
An army fighting for a cause, no matter what the cost

How many were returned to us at last from distant shore?
This bold red poppy stands alone for those that went before

Trish Abbott

Symphony Of Sunrise

New dawn is slowly breaking as the sunlight shows its face
Beyond a grey horizon it shines light towards this place
And golden warmth is spreading out across the rolling tide
It illuminates the frothy shores where darkness tries to hide

The shadows from the landscape brings an interesting view
Where the ever changing sky reveals a muted turquoise hue
While a jutting rock at water's edge reflects a silver sheen
As moistened salty crystals, add some sparkle to the scene

See rays of yellow sunlight fall upon the crests of waves
That splash upon the shingle as the water misbehaves
And as the bubbling foam pulls back into the briny sea
We can hear a special symphony of music wild and free

Trish Abbott

Wise Standing Tree

Stands alone beneath the stars, silhouettes the night time sky
Brittle fingers hold the moon to stop the time from passing by

Tall and noble, stout and strong many years this oak has seen
Roots hold firm beneath the earth that feeds the boughs and leaves of green

Birds have used him as their homes, sheltered from the winds and rain
Generations fledged and flown, return each year to start again

But as with life there follows death, making way for saplings new
Light returns to shadowed earth, bringing forth a different view

Trish Abbott

Firework's Night

Bright and sparkly fireworks are lighting up the sky

I'm thinking of the animals that are living so close by

Whizzes, pops and screeches, can be a child's delight

But very loud and frightening for creatures in the night

Rockets soaring in the sky with coloured starlight trails

Exploding down with golden rain and spiral crackling tails

We see the colours light the sky, hear pops and bangs galore

But our little dog is quivering and cowering on the floor

Outside the animals blindly run, they know not where to go

And little rabbits huddle close in burrows deep below

So spare a thought for those who share this earth on which we live

And keep our pets and creatures safe, around November 5th

Trish Abbott

Eventide

The sun has almost disappeared and leaves a warming glow behind

The trees just darkened shadows in the foreground of the pale skyline

The birds seek out their resting place preparing for the night ahead

And as the colours fade away it shrouds us in its velvet bed

One by one, the twinkling stars will grace us with their shining light

Oh how the picture changes as the eventide becomes the night

Trish Abbott

A Festive View

White frosty boughs are frozen on trees

as snowflakes fall on a sharp icy breeze

The tree lights twinkle and the baubles shine,

it's time for glasses of spicy mulled wine

The warming red glow from the fireside bright,

the singing of carols by soft candlelight

The fragrance of pine from the tall Christmas tree,

where stockings are hung for Santa to see

Children peer out through the window at night,

they hope for a glimpse of the sleigh so bright

But Santa wont stop (or so it's been said)

until they're tucked up and asleep in their bed

The mince pies are cooling a fragrance so sweet,

the table is laden with goodies to eat

And the mistletoe hangs in a place not to miss;

as we stand underneath with the hope of a kiss

Reflections Of Life

A dog stretches out on the fireside mat,

beside him the purrs of a warm sleeping cat

Try to imagine, and please do believe,

this view could be yours on this Christmas Eve

Trish Abbott

Christmas Joy

Dark clouds all heavy and full up with snow
waiting to fall on the land far below
Sprinkling down like a sugary dust,
covering paths with a crispy white crust
Footprints appear on the cold frosty ground.
Animals run but they don't make a sound
Looking for shelter in hedges and trees,
hiding away from the cold winter breeze

Warm fires burning with crackling logs,
a welcoming place for the old sleeping dogs
Stretching right out on the fireside mat,
leaving no room for the poor tired cat
Who picks out a spot on a nearby chair,
and licks at her paw with a haughty cold stare
But soon she curls up by the fireside bright,
giving in to the warmth and the soft golden light

Scent of the pine from the fresh Christmas tree,

while its twinkling lights so joyful to see

A small glass of sherry sits with a mince pie,

a tipple for Santa high up in the sky

While the choir below sing a beautiful song,

and the melody flows as we all sing along

A picture so festive and full of good cheer,

wishing all a great Yule and a peaceful new year

Trish Abbott

Thoughts Of Spring

The sun comes out each morning sending golden shafts on crisp white snow
And tiny glittering diamonds shine like sparkling jewels in the silvery glow
The bright blue sky so dazzling reflects upon the leaves of green
While little snowy crystal caps hide branches that remained unseen

And in the darkness creatures hide, their tell tale prints the only clue
While sheltering in the leafy mould, a tasty shoot they find to chew
A blackbird, dark amidst the white who cocks his head and looks around
He pecks at crumbs and bits of food we carefully scattered on the ground

As icicles thaw, they weep and melt while cleansing teardrops fall to earth
They splash in tiny pools below, which soak the seeds to start re-birth
And clumps of glistening snowdrop bloom to greet us on the sunny day
Their tiny heads nod back and forth as gentle breezes make them sway

And pretty soon spring will arrive, as seasons forge their natural course
New life, new growth, a change of scene replenishing the energy force
I gaze upon this snowy scene, and capture views before they fade
And give my thanks for nature's gift, a picture book of memories made

Trish Abbott

Views of Morning Mist

Along the misty road we see the dawning of the day

Shadows of the distant trees invites us "*walk this way*"

Sunrise lifts above the clouds and greets us with her glow

Rays of light reflecting gold to warm the fields below

As birds begin to wake and rise we hear their morning song

They call to greet each other while we slowly walk along

And we can almost feel the damp is lifting from the land

The promise of some winter sun to give the crops a hand

A better place to live and breathe, it would be hard to find

While pausing to enjoy the view, we leave the world behind

Trish Abbott

Greeting From The Sun

A welcome smile of sunrise sends a greeting on this day

There's beauty in the orange globe that melts the clouds away

While shadows at the water's edge reflect a softened hue

The stems of wispy grasses cling to early morning dew

I listen to the eerie calls of nature's feathered friends

Announcing all around them that the night is at an end

Then taking flight from branches of their safely roosting trees

They glide across the morning sky with gentle poise and ease

I feel the warmth upon my face while bathed in amber glow

So lost within the moment of this natural picture show

And just for one split second I am one with sky and ground

Embraced within its beauty as I softly gaze around

Trish Abbott

Just Waiting

Winter days seem long and dark, no warming sunshine glow
The thick grey clouds so dull and cold, bring icy sleet and snow
We gaze in hope for brighter days, when shoots push up their heads
And snowdrops come up one by one, from out of snowy beds

And when we have a sunny day, the colours seem so bright
The sky seems bluer somehow, and the stars shine more at night
As each day moves towards the spring look out for signs to see
A crocus head in melted snow, while buds form on the trees

Longer days, and shorter nights bring hopes of summer sun
And although the earth seems shrouded now, new life has just begun
Beneath the warmth of leafy moulds new shoots unfold and grow
And pretty soon they'll greet the day, bright colours all to show

So for now we wait, and look for signs, and keep the cold at bay
With curling smoke from chimney tops as fires warm our day
And when the birds start building nests, another sign for sure
That winter's past, and spring has come to knock upon our door

Trish Abbott

Prostate Cancer Support

Welcome to this lovely group we'd rather not be in
But cruel cancer finds us so it's here that we begin
A caring group of people who face journeys of their own
That will always pull together so you'll never feel alone

And if you're sad and in the dumps, a cheery voice will say
It really is quite normal that you feel like this today
A few will maybe crack a joke that makes you laugh and smile
To lighten up the heavy load you've carried for some while

But somehow at our darkest times when all we feel is fear
A gentle word to let you know a friend is always near
Advice is offered freely and the stories that we share
Brings familiar situations that so many can compare

While most still fight this battle sadly others will have lost
We have to carry on for them no matter what the cost
Lets' form a virtual circle together hand in hand
That brings comfort, strength and friendship to the men folk of this land

Trish Abbott

True Love

Being with you is a wonderful thing,
It makes me smile and makes me sing

With you beside me I feel proud
You stand out far beyond the crowd

I feel the warmth of your hand in mine
A smile from you and I feel fine

My heart beats strong and oh so fast
My love for you I know will last

I wanted to tell you how much I care
My true soul mate, I'll always be there

Trish Abbott

(It's called simply) **A Poem For You**

There is a shiny silver cord that joins your soul to mine

It keeps us close together, round our hearts it does entwine

And even though you journey on you're always here with me

Your broken body left behind, your spirit flying free

This special love is ours alone, no one can take away

With memories that I'll cherish with every passing day

I'll live this life the best I can, with dignity and pride

Until once more we find ourselves forever side by side

Trish Abbott

Morning Thoughts Of You

When I awaken every day your face is what I see
Those eyes that sparkle like the stars are looking up at me
A smile that says "I love you" lingers soft upon your lips
And hands that rest upon your cheek entwine your finger tips

The early morning sunshine bathes you in its golden light
It spreads its warmth and brightness to release the cold of night
While the silhouettes behind you slowly move across the wall
They breathe life into your features as they gently rise and fall

Your body that was so alive now sits behind a frame
Upon a wooden surface, where the memories remain
So at the dawn of every day my sadness I won't hide
Until once more I find myself forever by your side

Trish Abbott

The Empty Chair

In the corner of the garden room there stands an empty chair
The seat that once was occupied no longer holds you there
You said it was so comfy, such a lovely place to be
I'd look to see you dozing with our dog upon your knee

The stool that stands beside the chair to make the pair complete
Has lost the indentations where you used to rest your feet
And the table on the other side now has a vacant space
Just a pattern on the coaster where your cup you used to place

We used to sit and watch the birds that flew in every day
Now a Robin comes to visit since you had to go away
He cocks his head and looks across as if to say "hello"
Then perches on the garden fork to watch the ground below

We'd sit and chat for hours when I shared this room with you
And had private conversations that no others ever knew
The place is now so quiet, no more secrets to be told
No future plans between us, it's just me that's growing old

In the corner of the garden room the empty chair's still there

The seat gets dusted regularly with cherished love and care

And although no longer occupied it looks so right to see

It fills the corner of the room where once you used to be

Trish Abbott

Living With Grief

How does grief affect you? As far as I can tell
It's like being shut in prison in a solitary cell
On waking every morning, you decide today's the day
The feeling that you have the strength to push those clouds away

A memory distracts you and you're back to feeling weak
And the effort that it takes you just to walk, or think, or speak
It leaves you feeling hopeless as the tears begin to fall
So very overwhelming and it's not like you at all

When people ask you how you are, you smile and say "alright"
"It's been some time so really dear you should be feeling bright"
But deep inside your broken heart you know will never heal
It is easier saying "I'm ok" no matter how you feel

And places that you used to go together side by side
Are different when you're on your own it cannot be denied
Your heart is smashed to pieces that no hope will ever mend
A hundred letters written but with no address to send

Reflections Of Life

While sitting down and dozing in your favourite comfy chair

You dream you are together, and the happy times you share

Of course when you awaken you find yourself alone

The pain is overwhelming as you know you're on your own

And things that once excited you are now so dull instead

The loneliness is dreadful as you face an empty bed

So you lay there in the darkness as sleep won't come at all

While shapes that catch your vision gently move across the wall

It's here you have a private chat and maybe shed a tear

The things you'd do together, if only you were here

At some point you can hear the birds that sing at early light

Another day approaches after one more sleepless night

So up you get, you wash and dress, not caring what you wear

Then look into the mirror at the stranger standing there

You promise that today shall be a day that you wont hide

That's just a tiny part of grief and how you feel inside

Perhaps today

Trish Abbott

Just A Matter Of Time

How can it be a year has passed, it seems just like one day

How quickly time has travelled since you had to go away

My broken heart feels empty I still struggle with the pain

To have you back within my arms, to hold you once again

But we know it cannot happen, I accept that you have gone

And the promises I made to you, I will carry out alone

Continuing without you sadly I don't have a choice

I often hear your laughter and the echo of your voice

With pictures placed around the house I see your smiling face

That bond we have (*the silver thread*) is strongly still in place

My precious friend, my life, my love, forever in my heart

Sweet memories I'll keep right there while we remain apart

So if healing is a journey then a mountain I must climb

I will reach the top eventually; it's just a matter of time

Trish Abbott

Beautiful Jess

(6 Jan 1999 – 17 July 2013)

To some it's just a dog you see

Nothing special, except to me

A friend beside me through the years

Always there to dry my tears

So pleased to see me every day

A wagging tail, a ball to play

I look into those eyes now old

They used to be so bright and bold

The way you beg for things to eat

And ask us for that special treat

To see the way you run with glee

Across the meadows wild and free

And stretch out in a sunny place

The look of peace upon your face

When in the evenings on my lap

You curl up tight to take a nap

Reflections Of Life

I'll miss your tongue that licks my skin

The heart that holds the love within

Your trust in us without a fear

A faithful friend to have so near

It's just a dog, no special thing

Until you see what joy they bring.

Trish Abbott

Our Mate Spud

(22 July 2000 – 15 August 2016)

Spud never was the sharpest knife that lived in kitchen draw

But he turned out to be the one we always will adore

A funny clown that makes us smile when we are feeling blue

And follows like a shadow making sure we're just in view

I feel him lying at my feet when I sit down to write

He sighs to let me know he's there although he's out of sight

The funny way he lets us know he's ready for his bed

"It's biscuit time" he's telling us, though not a word is said

To see the joy shine from his eyes when we walk by the sea

With barks galore as stones are thrown; a happy dog is he

Just recently we noticed though, our boy is not himself

As illness and the years have taken toll upon his health

And now the time has come for us to say our last goodbyes

A heavy heart we have today as tears fall from our eyes

But he will go to join our Jess, no longer feeling pain

They'll run and play in fields of green, together once again

Trish Abbott

Tiny Footsteps Above

Imagine a special loving place where tiny babies play

Lots of giggling laughter and fun and games each day

It's always warm and sunny there where rainbows can be seen

The sky is blue with fluffy clouds; the soft grass is so green

And everywhere is safe to play there is no "out of bounds"

The soft melodic music plays with gentle angel sounds

All Illness is forgotten and all pain is left behind

A place where suffering is no more and lightness fills the mind

But up there high above the clouds they watch us here below

Sending tiny little feathers on the gentle breeze that blows

Or sometimes they send kisses that feel soft like a caress

Asking angels to protect us at our bedside while we rest

Printed in Great Britain
by Amazon